I Love You Niece Because

MW00915366

2021 Copyright © What I Love About Foxes Publishing

All rights reserved. This book or any portion thereof may not be reproduced or used in any manner in whatsoever without the express written permission of the publisher.

I Love Your

_____

You inspire me to

_____

I'M HUMBLED BY YOUR

_____

I LOVE HOW YOU ALWAYS

_____

I LOVE HOW YOU NEVER

_____

I LOVE REMEMBERING THE TIME WE WENT

_____

_____

If I had to describe you in one word it'd be

_____

You have the prettiest

_____

I love that you taught me

_____

I HAVE TO ADMIT YOU'RE ALWAYS RIGHT ABOUT

_____

I LOVE THAT YOU LOVE MY

_____

I admire your dedication to

_____

I love your taste in

_____

You are so

_____

_____

_____

I'D LOVE IT IF WE COULD

_____

I LOVE IT WHEN YOU CALL ME

_____

I LOVE HEARING STORIES ABOUT YOUR

_____

I never get tired of your

_____

IT MAKES ME SMILE WHEN YOU

_____

IT MAKES ME SMILE WHEN YOU

_____

Made in the USA
Coppell, TX
05 December 2024

41793001R00024